JANE

Starvation, Cannibalism, and Endurance at Jamestown

James Horn   William Kelso
Douglas Owsley   Beverly Straube

Acknowledgements

We would like to acknowledge the following, without whom this book and the broader project it is based on would have been impossible:

Mark J. and Loretta J. Roman for their generous support of the publication costs of this book.

Roy Hock and Margaret Fowler for their passion for archaeological research at James Fort and for underwriting Jane's facial reconstruction.

At the Smithsonian's National Museum of Natural History, for their outstanding forensic investigations, Dr. Douglas Owsley, Kari Bruwelheide, Bruno Frolich, Scott Whittaker, Don Hurlbert, Dr. Christine France, Nicole Little, Vicki Simon, and Cass Taylor.

Dr. Stephen Rouse for taking fragments and making them whole again, and Medical Modeling who produced stereolithograph casts of Jane, the base for the sculptors to build on. StudioEIS for bringing art and science together: Ivan Schwartz, Elliott Schwartz, BJ Ervik, Jiwoong Cheh, and Rebecca Spivack.

Aimee Kratts, for countless hours researching and working on the coif that covers Jane's head. Exhibit mounts were enhanced with the help of the Colonial Williamsburg Foundation's Exhibits Specialist Jim Armbruster. Sketches of the shoe were provided by Colonial Williamsburg Foundation Cordwainer Al Seguto. Zooarchaeological analysis was provided by Joanne Bowen and Susan Trevarthen Andrews.

Bermuda images were obtained with the help of Douglas Scott, Cabinet Office of Bermuda, and Andrew Baylay, Records Officer, Bermuda Archives. The image of bandoliers was provided courtesy of Wight N. Manning. All other images are credited to Charles Durfor, BJ Ervik, David Givens, Don Hurlbert, Michael Lavin, Adam Mead, and Mary Anna Richardson. The Sydney King painting is courtesy of the National Park Service, Colonial National Historical Park, Jamestown Collection.

The *Jamestown Rediscovery* team for the "find" and finding out: Jeff Aronowitz, Bentley Boyd, Charles Durfor, Dan Gamble, David Givens, Dr. James Horn, Dr. William Kelso, Michael Lavin, Jamie May, Sheryl Mays, Merry Outlaw, Mary Anna Richardson, Danny Schmidt, Dan Smith, Beverly Straube, Mark Summers, Don Warmke, Julie Zellers-Fredrick and Andrew Zellers-Fredrick. Special thanks to the 2012 Rediscovery Summer Field Institute and interns supported by a generous grant from Don and Elaine Bogus: Leah Stricker, Bob Chartrand, Lauren Menzer, and Micheal Rohrer.

We are grateful for the continued support of Preservation Virginia's Board of Trustees and Executive Director Elizabeth Kostelny in collaboration with The Colonial Williamsburg Foundation.

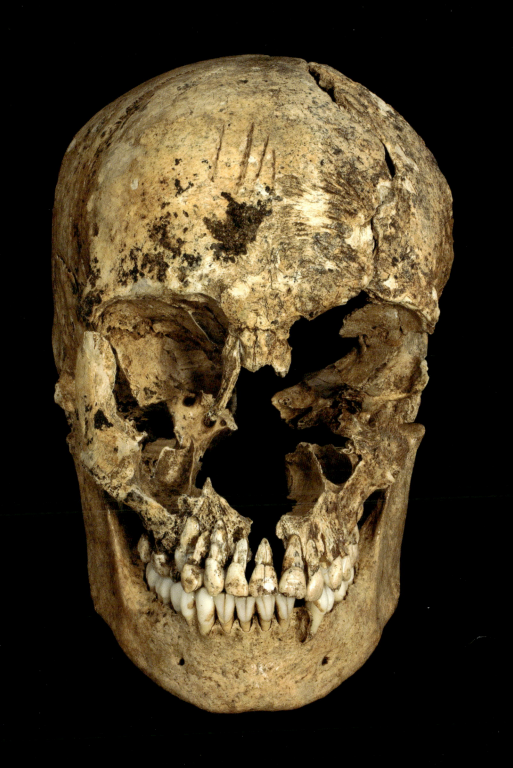

We Call Her Jane

We call her Jane: female, fourteen years old, possibly from southern England.

She left Plymouth, England, in June 1609 as part of the largest fleet yet to sail to the new colony of Virginia. But a terrifying hurricane scattered the fleet in the Atlantic and her ship eventually limped into Jamestown in mid-August. Less than a year later she was dead.

These are the things we know about her. There is much more we do not know. Who was she? Why did she leave home? Was she the daughter of a well-to-do family, or was she a humble maidservant? What were her hopes and aspirations in America? Was she timid in the face of the unknown, or was she brave and determined to start a new life? How did she die?

We know so little about Jane because like so many ordinary men, women, and children of the time she was not recorded in the historical documents. But today she is our only tangible human reminder of one of the darkest periods in Jamestown's history—the "starving time"—when in the winter months of 1609 and early spring of 1610 most of Jamestown's inhabitants died of sickness and starvation.

Archaeologists found Jane in 2012 in the cellar of an early James Fort building. She was not interred in a grave; instead her skull and a section of her leg bone were buried with pottery sherds, discarded weaponry, and other remnants of everyday life in the colony. The circumstances leading to her final resting place, however, were far from everyday.

Today, Jane's remains are being reconstructed by archaeologists, physical anthropologists, and artists. This is her story.

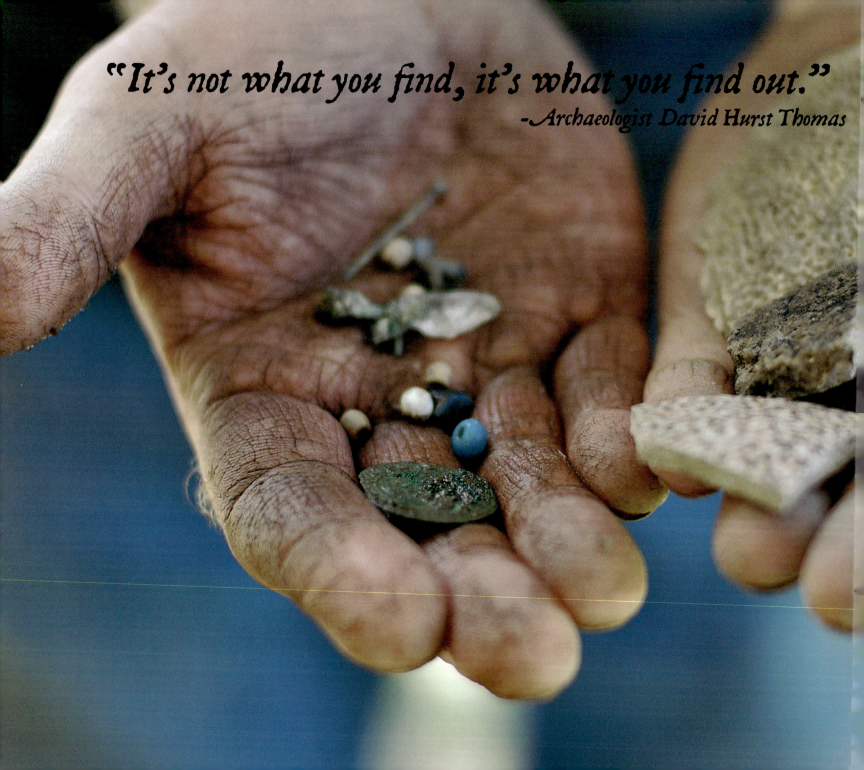

Jamestown was the first permanent English settlement in North America. Established in 1607, the colony survived wars with local Indian peoples (Powhatans), factionalism, famine, high rates of mortality, and a bitter internal rebellion. It saw the first meeting of a representative assembly in the Americas, the establishment of the first English Church, and arrival of the first enslaved Africans to Virginia. When a fire devastated government buildings at the end of the century and the capital moved to Williamsburg, however, the footprint of James Fort quickly faded from view.

The Association for the Preservation of Virginia Antiquities (now Preservation Virginia) acquired 22.5 acres on Jamestown Island in 1893 to protect the memory of America's birthplace. In 1994 the APVA began an archaeological project called *Jamestown Rediscovery* to find the remains of the original James Fort, ca. 1607–1624. Twenty years of exploration have established the location of the fort and principal buildings, and recovered more than 1.5 million artifacts. The project has rewritten our understanding of early settlers' daily life and purpose, their relations with Indian peoples, and revealed a narrative of human endeavor and perseverance that laid the foundations of British America and ultimately the United States.

Finding Jane

In April 2012, archaeologists with the *Jamestown Rediscovery* project returned to a cellar discovered in one of James Fort's earliest buildings. They had uncovered other cellars during two decades of investigation, and now their work revealed this underground L-shaped room had functioned as a kitchen. Objects in the cellar's backfill dirt indicated it was probably covered over as part of a general cleanup ordered in June 1610 by the colony's newly arrived governor, Sir Thomas West, the 12th Baron De La Warr.

Late one Friday afternoon, senior archaeologist Jamie May came to the project's director of archaeology, Dr. William Kelso, and told him of an intriguing discovery. An intern was uncovering what May thought looked like human teeth. Kelso was not immediately excited—the team had uncovered teeth and even partial skulls before in other early 17th-century deposits. Human remains were sometimes found with discarded artifacts as a result of later settlers accidently digging into one of the hundreds of unmarked burials scattered across the fort site.

To see the find for himself, Kelso climbed down the original clay steps that settlers had built into the cellar. In the dirt were indeed human teeth, as well as butchered animal bones and artifacts dating to the dark days of 1609–1610, known as the "starving time." Because the workweek was coming to an end, the team carefully reburied the teeth and waited through a long weekend to restart a more intensive excavation.

That excavation proved extraordinary. In addition to the teeth, archaeologists found half a human skull and other fragmented cranial remains. In the same fill layer as the skull, the upper end of a right tibia appeared. There were indications that the skull had been chopped in two. Was this blow the cause of death—evidence of a 400-year-old murder? Or was it a sign of something else, even more startling?

Jane's Context

Where human bones are discovered can tell investigators a lot about the circumstances of the person's life and death. Most of the artifacts found in the L-shaped cellar dated to a time after the building had stopped being used for its original purpose. As the building above it fell down and timbers rotted away, the cellar became a useful hole into which the colonists could put trash.

Jane's cellar, designated Structure 191, contained over 47,000 artifacts. They were the types of materials the *Jamestown Rediscovery* team had recovered from other areas filled when Lord De La Warr arrived in the colony and ordered the rebuilding of the fort. Such objects include military equipment, Indian pots that had been used by the colonists, ceramics designed for metallurgical purposes, and numerous glass trade beads.

Confirmation of the cellar's ca. 1610 date of fill was found in the ceramic crossmends senior curator Bly Straube was able to make. Crossmending means that pottery sherds from one feature of the fort match pottery sherds from another, and this establishes a relationship between the two. An example of this from Jane's cellar is the medallion of a German stoneware Bartmann jug which mended to the rest of the jug found in a nearby well that had been filled with trash in 1610.

The top portion of this German stoneware jug was found in a well (1608–1610) adjacent to the cellar. The medallion (center) was found in the same context as Jane.

This fragmented clay pot was found next to Jane's remains. Characteristic of Virginia Indian pottery, this may have been produced specifically for use by James Fort colonists.

"What will it availe you to take that by force you may quickly have by love, or to destroy them that provide you food[?]"
—Powhatan to John Smith 1608

Other clues indicating that the cellar was filled in 1610 come from studying faunal material—the bones of animals and shells of mollusks. The chronological markers for this discovery are two major historical events that occurred before Lord De La Warr's arrival at Jamestown.

From the very first months of the colony, the Jamestown settlers had a hard time feeding themselves. Captain John Smith's skill at trading European goods for Virginia Indian corn kept the colony going in its first years. But then damage to a large supply fleet from England in the summer of 1609 put a strain on the colony.

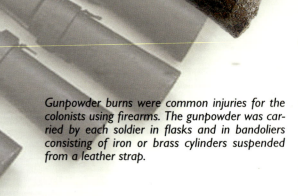

Gunpowder burns were common injuries for the colonists using firearms. The gunpowder was carried by each soldier in flasks and in bandoliers consisting of iron or brass cylinders suspended from a leather strap.

The new settlers who came on the damaged ships ate through the colony's seven acres of planted corn in three days. A month later a mysterious gunpowder explosion severely injured Smith, who had been acting president of the colony at that time, and forced him to return to London.

A severe drought, damage to the large supply fleet that left England in June 1609, and deteriorating relations with the Powhatans, partly caused by the settlers' demands on them for food, put an enormous strain on the colony.

The 300 settlers crowded into James Fort faced the coming winter with fractured leadership, insufficient provisions, and the imminent prospect of war with the hostile Powhatans who surrounded them. Placed under siege by the Indians, the colonists could not safely venture outside of the fort's walls to find food in the woods or along the river. In desperation, colonists resorted to eating snakes, rats, cats, and their dogs and horses. They even boiled shoe leather for sustenance. Recent faunal analysis of the L-shaped cellar by zooarchaeologists Joanne Bowen and Susan Andrews confirmed evidence of butchered dog and horse bones.

Coffin bone from a horse's hoof (top) and dog mandible found in "starving time" contexts.

A collection of faunal remains from the "John Smith" well (1608–1610). The volume and range of animals consumed, such as rats and snakes, paint a grim picture of the beginning of the "starving time."

The George Somers map of Bermuda (ca. 1609).

The second chronological marker is related to the first. The end of the "starving time" was brought about by the unexpected but welcome appearance in May 1610 of survivors of the *Sea Venture* shipwreck in Bermuda.

The *Sea Venture* was the flagship of the great fleet of 1609. Commanded by Sir Thomas Gates and Sir George Somers, the fleet consisted of nine ships carrying supplies and more than 500 new colonists. When a massive tempest hit the fleet in the Atlantic, Somers stayed at the helm of the *Sea Venture*, which suffered the brunt of the storm. The ship's crew and passengers became exhausted from bailing, and water had risen in the hold to nine feet when Somers spied Bermuda and deliberately drove his sinking vessel onto the reefs. In their ten months on the island, the 150 castaways built a church, houses, and two ships to carry them the rest of the way to Virginia.

The delayed settlers arrived in Virginia with seashells, sea turtles, and Bermudan sea birds and fish. They also ballasted their two small ships with Bermuda limestone. Some of the Bermudan seashells were tossed into the L-shaped cellar and were found by archaeologists 400 years later.

Artifacts from Bermuda found in James Fort contexts: Top shell (top), queen conch shell (middle), and Bermuda limestone (bottom).

A block of soil containing Jane's remains was taken to the archaeologist's Rediscovery Center laboratory for careful cleaning and investigation. In this controlled environment, micro tools, picks, and brushes were used to avoid marring the surface of the bones with blemishes that could be misinterpreted as bone trauma made at the time of death. The humidity of the workplace is also monitored closely so that bones do not dry too quickly and then crack or peel when the dirt that had covered them for 400 years is removed.

As the cleaning progressed, the *Jamestown Rediscovery* conservators noticed several abnormal marks. Chop marks were revealed on the forehead and back of the cranium.

The staff immediately sought assistance from the Smithsonian Institution's bone experts. Dr. Douglas Owsley, forensic anthropologist and Division Head for Physical Anthropology at the Smithsonian's National Museum of Natural History, has worked for years with law enforcement agencies on criminal cases. He and his team have also studied thousands of skeletons from the distant past. Now it was their turn to look at this evidence from the early 17th century.

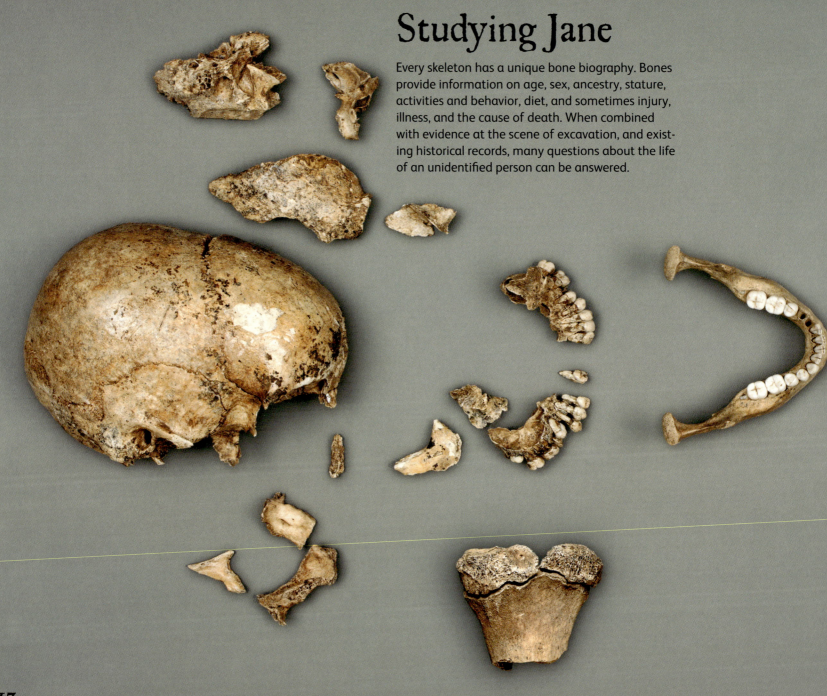

Studying Jane

Every skeleton has a unique bone biography. Bones provide information on age, sex, ancestry, stature, activities and behavior, diet, and sometimes injury, illness, and the cause of death. When combined with evidence at the scene of excavation, and existing historical records, many questions about the life of an unidentified person can be answered.

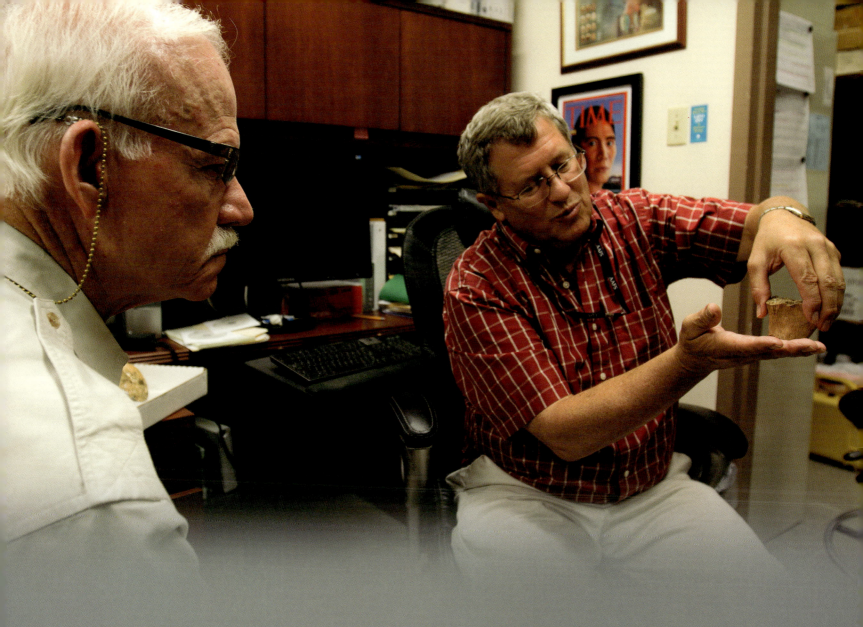

Over the past twenty years, Owsley and his team have examined many of the human remains found at Jamestown. One skeleton had been shot in the leg and another proved to be a young boy hit with an arrow in 1607. Smithsonian anthropologists also helped identify the remains of Captain Bartholomew Gosnold, a major planner of the colony. The expertise of Owsley's team has even aided in the facial reconstruction of early settlers, based on skull morphology (features) and the story written in their bones.

Age

The growth and development of teeth and bones provide reliable markers for the age of an individual. Teeth develop at relatively standard rates. Deciduous (baby) teeth are present through childhood and are replaced with permanent teeth. The third molars (wisdom teeth) are the last to form. By age 13 their roots are starting to develop, but they are not fully erupted from the mandible (jaw) until about age 18.

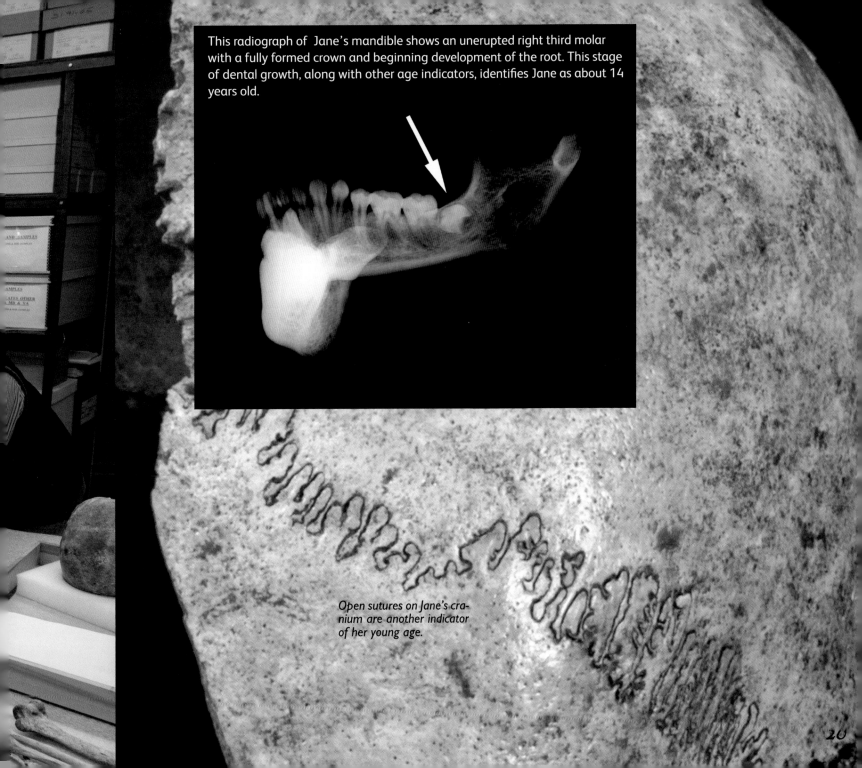

This radiograph of Jane's mandible shows an unerupted right third molar with a fully formed crown and beginning development of the root. This stage of dental growth, along with other age indicators, identifies Jane as about 14 years old.

Open sutures on Jane's cranium are another indicator of her young age.

Male or Female?

Cranial shape can be an indicator of sex. Females tend to have a smooth, vertical forehead, whereas males tend to have a lower, sloping forehead and a more strongly developed brow ridge.

Just behind the openings of the ear canals are anatomical protrusions of bone known as the mastoid processes—attachment areas for neck muscles that are usually smaller in females.

Near the base of the posterior cranium is a ridge of bone that serves as an attachment area for strong neck muscles. Females tend to exhibit less development of this nuchal ridge in comparison to males. This gives the female cranium a smoother, rounded appearance.

Smithsonian's Kari Bruwelheide fits a piece of Jane's cranium back into place.

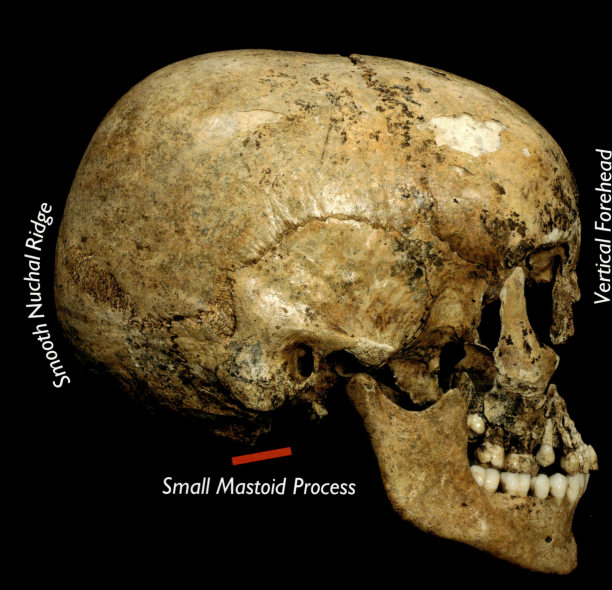

Smooth Nuchal Ridge

Vertical Forehead

Small Mastoid Process

Origins

Skeletal features, especially the shape of the skull, provide clues to ancestry. As part of assessing the human remains found at Jamestown, Owsley and his team have examined and measured crania at the University of Cambridge in England. This British collection and other reference collections of 17th-century skeletons provide useful comparative data for determining the origins of early immigrants to the New World.

Additional information about an individual's country of origin come from isotopic testing. Stored within bone are chemical signatures that contain heavy oxygen ($\delta^{18}O$), nitrogen ($\delta^{15}N$), and carbon ($\delta^{13}C$) isotopes. Some of these data are locked into our skeletal structure from our drinking water (the oxygen isotope signature) as we mature. Carbon and nitrogen isotope values reflect the different types of foods consumed and incorporated into the body's tissues.

Oxygen isotopes from the environment are stored in our teeth in childhood and can be used with other information to determine where a person grew up. Because bones remodel with age, the carbon isotope signature from foods can change, providing an indication of how long an individual lived in North America. This shift is recognizable because there are differences in the isotope values of New World (corn) versus Old World (wheat and barley) crops. These different types of plants have different isotope values, which are evident in the consumers, both livestock and humans, of these foods. A person's status can also be inferred from isotope analysis since stable isotope nitrogen values allow interpretation of the relative amounts of protein in one's diet.

Jane's isotopic values told the story of a mid- to upper-class individual born along the coastal plains of southern England and recently arrived at Jamestown. Does this profile indicate that Jane was a high-status individual, or may she have been a maidservant eating the same food as those she served? Jane's results are just one more piece of the rich narrative that describes our nation's very beginnings.

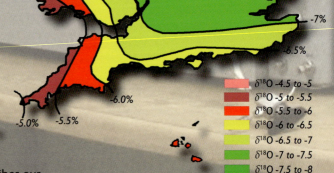

Dr. Christine France stands next to the equipment used to measure Jane's isotopic signatures. Isotopic map of England (left). Jane's signature indicated she was from the costal plains (yellow banding).

$\delta^{18}O$ -4.5 to -5
$\delta^{18}O$ -5 to -5.5
$\delta^{18}O$ -5.5 to -6
$\delta^{18}O$ -6 to -6.5
$\delta^{18}O$ -6.5 to -7
$\delta^{18}O$ -7 to -7.5
$\delta^{18}O$ -7.5 to -8
$\delta^{18}O$ -8 to -8.5
$\delta^{18}O$ -8.5 to -9

Evidence of Survival Cannibalism

Smithsonian's Scott Whittaker inspects Jane's mandible under stereo-zoom microscopy.

Dog bones from "starving time" contexts show clear and concise chops.

Under magnification, Jane's mandible shows close-interval cut marks indicative of sawing motions with a very sharp knife.

Of the many tools that a forensic anthropologist has at their disposal, often the most useful is magnification. Magnifying lenses, stereo-zoom microscopes, and even scanning electron microscopes (SEM) are used to see what the naked eye cannot. Although the form of some of the microscopes has not changed in centuries, modern technology with automation and digital cameras has transformed them into precise instruments that often illuminate unseen evidence.

Under magnification, Jane's mandible tells a very interesting forensic story. Multiple, fine cuts on the jaw showed not only that a very sharp knife was used, but that the cutting was often done in quick sawing motions. Nearly imperceptible knife jabs to the bottom of the jaw clearly indicate intent to remove flesh.

Was this act committed by someone familiar with the butchering of animals, or was this person hesitant in completing this grisly task? Forensic anthropologists turned to processed animal bones found in the same contexts as Jane. Under magnification, it is clear that the cuts in the butchered animal bones were made with a more forceful and patterned execution suggesting a very different method from the processing marks in the human bone.

After studying the remains from the L-shaped cellar, the Smithsonian forensic anthropologists confirmed the archaeology team's suspicions: the remains had been cut up for food (cannibalized). The skull and leg bone had undergone sustained blows. The chops and cuts from several sharp, metal implements reflected a concerted effort to separate the brain and soft tissue from bone.

How did Owsley and his team determine that post mortem butchering of the skull and leg is evidence of cannibalism?

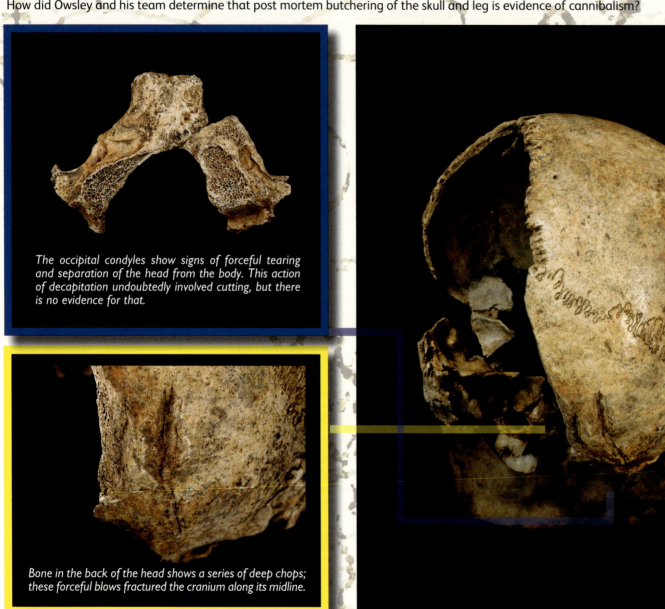

The occipital condyles show signs of forceful tearing and separation of the head from the body. This action of decapitation undoubtedly involved cutting, but there is no evidence for that.

Bone in the back of the head shows a series of deep chops; these forceful blows fractured the cranium along its midline.

Four chops to the middle forehead represent a tentative, failed attempt to open the cranium.

Bone below the right eye socket (maxilla) has a series of small, fine cuts from a knife used to remove cheek muscles.

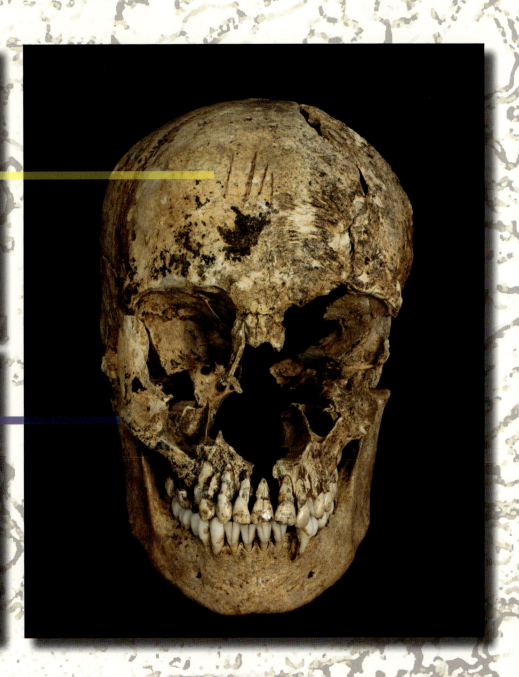

The left temporal bone was punctured by a small tool with a rectangular profile. The narrow edge of the tool caused this compression fracture as it pried the bone from the side of the head to gain access to the brain.

Numerous small knife cuts and punctures in the mandible reflect attempts to remove tissues from both the inside and outside of the lower jaw.

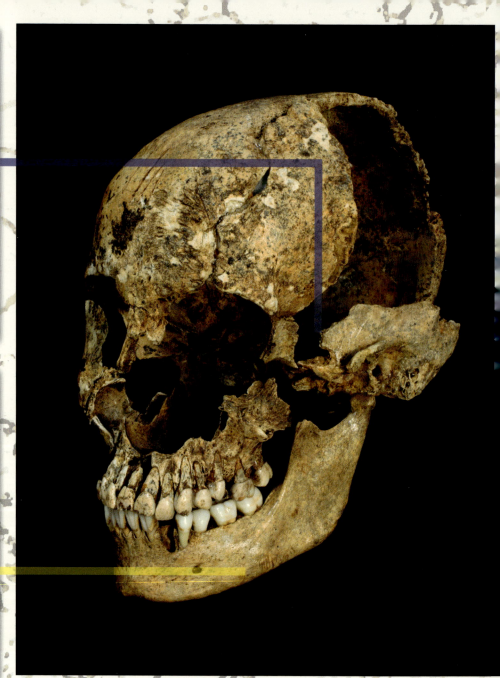

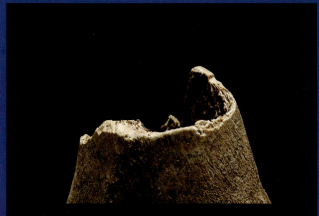

The right tibia bone has a chop halfway through its shaft. The blade entered the leg bone below the knee and from behind, breaking the shaft and exposing the marrow.

Extremely fine cuts near the chop indicate a sharp knife was also used to remove the leg.

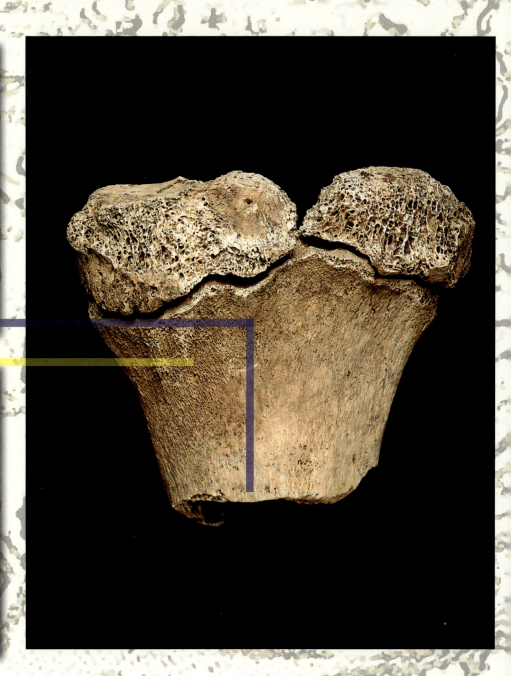

Jane's Winter at Jamestown

The winter of 1609–1610 was a profound crisis for the colonists crowded into James Fort and a turning point in the colony's history. It proved a harrowing test of the settlers' endurance and will to live.

After Captain John Smith's departure from Jamestown in October 1609, leadership fell to George Percy, one of the original gentry settlers of the colony. Shortly after he took over, a full-scale war broke out with the Powhatans and the Indians organized a siege of the fort, effectively cutting off the colonists from any hope of outside relief. The rapidly dwindling supplies and unsanitary conditions of the overcrowded fort soon began to cause starvation and the spread of disease.

As the Indians' siege continued and winter set in, severe hunger drove the colonists to desperation. Percy wrote that starving settlers dug up "dead corpses outt of graves" and ate them. Others "Licked upp the Bloode w[hi]ch ha[d] fallen from their weake fellowes." One of the settlers allegedly murdered his pregnant wife "as she slept in his bosome," then "Ripped the childe outt of her woambe and threw itt into the River and after chopped the Mother in pieces and salted her for his foode."

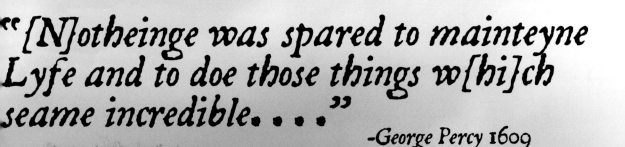

"[N]otheinge was spared to mainteyne Lyfe and to doe those things w[hi]ch seame incredible...."

—George Percy 1609

"The human consumption of human flesh is as old as mankind," historian Mark Nicholls reminds us. Societies across the world from prehistoric times have adopted the practice either for ritualistic or other reasons. Powdered human bones and human blood, for example, were widely believed to have potent medicinal benefits and were used by all sections of European society in the 16th and 17th centuries.

But the consumption of human flesh at Jamestown was neither ritualistic nor medicinal. It was for survival. The terrible suffering and psychological trauma caused by prolonged starvation together with the will to survive induced settlers "to doe those things w[hi]ch seame incredible As to digge up dead corpses outt of graves and to eate them."

Jamestown was not the only colony to endure such privations and not the only place where European settlers turned to cannibalism out of sheer desperation. In early Spanish colonies on the River Plate and in the Straits of Magellan, settlers also resorted to eating human flesh when there appeared no hope of relief. In 1649, a group of English settlers marooned on an island off the Eastern Shore of Virginia were reduced to living off those who died. There are many tales of survivors at sea who ate their fellows as a last resort. More recent are the examples of the Donner Party in the American West of the mid-19th century and of the survivors of the Andes plane crash in South America in 1972.

At what point Jane died during that terrible winter we do not know. Possibly her family had already perished, and when she died, with no one to look after her, the remains of her body were taken up and eaten as a despairing last resort by one or more of the dwindling survivors.

Jamestown after Jane

The "starving time" reduced the James Fort population from approximately 300 to barely 60, "The reste beinge either sterved throwe famin or cutt of by the Salvages."

When he eventually arrived from Bermuda in late May 1610, Sir Thomas Gates was appalled by the conditions. The palisades of the fort had been torn down, the church was ruined, and empty houses "rent up and burnt." The fort's survivors were described as "Lamentable to behowlde." Those able to raise themselves from their beds to meet Gates and his men "Looked Lyke Anotamies" [skeletons]. They cried out, "we are starved We are starved." Yet Gates could do little to help them. He had brought only limited stores from Bermuda for his own people. There was no hope of getting any food from the Powhatans or any means of taking fish from the rivers in sufficient quantities to keep the colonists alive.

Horrified at the terrible suffering he witnessed, Gates decided to abandon the colony. To the great joy of the ragged Jamestown survivors, he announced the decision to return to England. Discharging a doleful volley of small shot by way of farewell, the colonists set off in their ships at midday on June 7, 1610, heading for the mouth of the Chesapeake Bay and the Atlantic Ocean. Seemingly, the Jamestown colony was at an end.

Portrait of Sir Thomas Gates as it hangs in the Cabinet Office in Bermuda.

Ivory pocket sundial found in the same layer as Jane's remains.

Cahow leg bones from James Fort. Native to the islands of Bermuda, this docile bird was preyed upon by shipwrecked colonists and prepared as food for the voyage to Virginia in 1610.

In a turnaround of truly heroic proportions, however, Gates and the colonists got no farther than a dozen miles down-river. Waiting for the tide to turn, Gates's company spotted a boat making towards them—an advance party of a relief expedition led by the colony's new Governor General, Lord De La Warr, which had recently entered the Bay with three ships and 150 colonists. From being on the brink of collapse, the colony now had a full complement of leaders, some 390 settlers, and plenty of provisions.

Jamestown's survival had been little short of miraculous.

De La Warr's timely arrival did not bring a lasting improvement in the colony's fortunes. The next fifteen years would continue to be challenging as the colonists tried to make Virginia profitable and struggled to establish themselves in the face of continuing fierce resistance from the Powhatans. But never again would the colony come so close to being abandoned.

Seeing Jane

Early 17th-century engraving of a woman wearing a bodkin by Wenceslaus Hollar.

We will probably never know Jane's true identity, but the biographies of the women who are recorded as venturing to Virginia around 1610 are revealing. From the records we know of at least six and possibly seven females who were present during the horrific events of the "starving time," but there must have been more. By combining archival documentation with the data gathered through the forensic studies of Jane's remains, we have learned a lot about her.

Most of the women who arrived in Jamestown during the early years were the wives or daughters of gentlemen or were maidservants. This pattern was repeated among the five known women onboard the *Sea Venture* who were shipwrecked on Bermuda.

Children, like women, are rarely mentioned in the historical record of Jamestown; but based on artifacts they left behind, such as shoes and toys, we know they had arrived by early 1610.

Is it possible to know what Jane looked like?

Silver bodkins. These artifacts are rare evidence of women's presence at Jamestown.

Silver child's teething stick and whistle found in a post "starving time" context.

Parts of a childs' leather shoe found in the well of 1611.

36

The underlying bone structure of the skull determines individual appearance more than most people imagine. However, reconstructing a face from the pieces of skull that once supported it requires skill in both art and science. In rebuilding Jane's appearance, multiple experts formed a team that put the pieces of her skull back together, interpreted the unique characteristics in her bones, and revived her image from four centuries ago.

The skull was rebuilt using computed tomography, or CT scanning, and computer imaging software. A CT scan of each of the skull fragments gave 3-D medical modeling expert Dr. Stephen Rouse a digital representation of exactly what one sees if holding the bone in hand. Rouse virtually rebuilt the broken skull using the virtual bone models. Computer software allowed missing parts of the skull to be created by copying bones that did survive on the opposite side and then reversed those pieces. With such mirror imaging, the skull was aligned to approach its pre-death shape.

In that way, cranial bone from Jane's missing left side was filled in. The fracture in the middle of her skull was digitally corrected and her bones returned to their proper anatomical position.

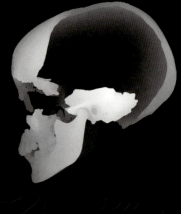
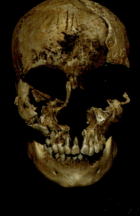
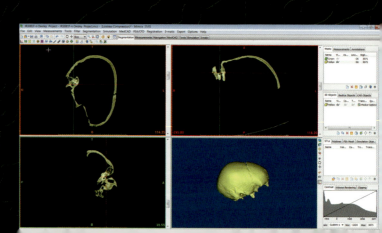

Dr. Stephen Rouse (top) works to reconstruct Jane's fragmented cranium. CT images of Jane from which a resin cast was made for facial reconstruction (bottom right). Three-dimensional images created from the scanned fragments (right). Actual images of the bone were applied to the surface of the model (bottom left).

The Smithsonian team meets with the StudioEIS team to discuss the Jane project.

The initial resin cast of Jane's skull.

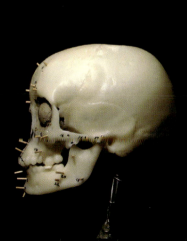
Tissue depth markers matching Jane's age, sex, and ancestry are added.

Douglas Owsley discusses cranial morphology with sculptor Jiwoong Cheh.

From Dr. Rouse's work, a detailed resin cast can be made of Jane's cranium. Using the skull cast, Owsley and Bruwelheide from the Smithsonian consult with sculptors from StudioEIS, a firm specializing in lifelike casts of historical figures. Together they attempt to create a forensic facial reconstruction of Jane that is both biologically and historically accurate.

The initial resin cast.

StudioEIS sculptor Jiwoong Cheh adds clay to the resin cast.

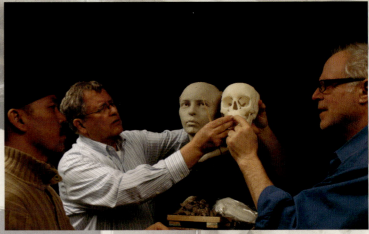
Dr. Owsley, Cheh, and Ivan Schwartz assess the nearly complete model.

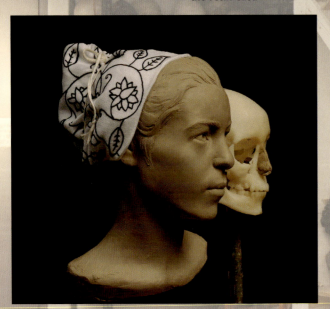
Jane's profile next to her resin cast.

StudioEIS artist Rebecca Spivack applies flesh tones to Jane's reconstruction.

Once clay has been added to the cast, Cheh works and reworks the face in consultation with the Smithsonian anthropologists, who point out individual characteristics expressed in the underlying bone. Features related to age and body position are incorporated into the figure, as are eye and hair color and hair style. Seventeenth-century portraits and clothing patterns provide useful references, and helped determine Jane's headdress or "coif." Not readily available today except in museum and private collections, the coif had to be hand made by a costume researcher specializing in late 16th- and early 17th-century apparel.

JANE 1596-1610

Endurance

The story told by Jane's remains is of Jamestown's darkest hours. Tragically, she and more than two hundred colonists perished during that terrible winter, some so driven by hunger that they ate their dead compatriots in a desperate effort to survive.

Even though most of the colonists died during the winter of 1609–1610, the colony endured, and by enduring had a profound influence on the future of America. In time, Virginia would develop as the wealthiest and most populous of the British mainland colonies—the first transoceanic site of an empire that would carry the English language, laws, institutions, and the Protestant Church across North America and the globe.

Representative government, founded at Jamestown in 1619, would blossom into a vibrant political culture and spread throughout the British colonies, leading (in a different age) to a new republican credo that would be expressed in the founding of the United States.